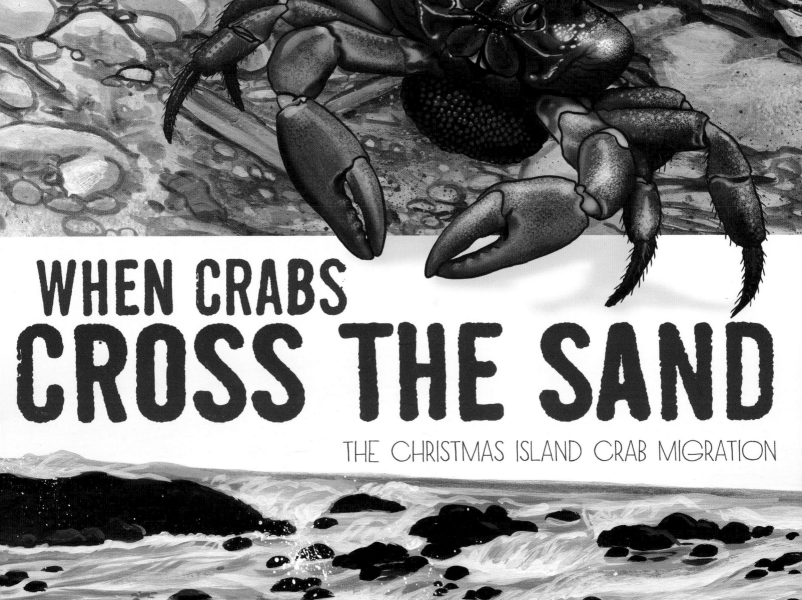

WHEN CRABS CROSS THE SAND

THE CHRISTMAS ISLAND CRAB MIGRATION

BY SHARON KATZ COOPER

ILLUSTRATED BY CHRISTINA WALD

PICTURE WINDOW BOOKS
a capstone imprint

Thanks to our advisers for their expertise, research, and advice:

Elizabeth Davis-Berg, PhD, Associate Professor of Biology
Columbia College Chicago

Terry Flaherty, PhD, Professor of English
Minnesota State University, Mankato

Editor: Jill Kalz
Designer: Lori Bye
Art Director: Nathan Gassman
Production Specialist: Laura Manthe
The illustrations in this book were created with acrylics.
Image Credit: Shutterstock: pavalena, 3 (map)

Picture Window Books are published by Capstone,
1710 Roe Crest Drive, North Mankato, Minnesota 56003
www.capstoneyoungreaders.com

Library of Congress Cataloging-in-Publication Data
Katz Cooper, Sharon, author.
  When crabs cross the sand : the Christmas Island crab migration / by
Sharon Katz Cooper ; illustrated by Christina Wald.
      pages cm.—(Nonfiction picture books. Extraordinary migrations
  Summary: "Follows a single Christmas Island crab on its annual
migration journey"—Provided by publisher.
  Audience: K to grade 3.
  Includes bibliographical references and index.
  ISBN 978-1-4795-6077-6 (library binding)
  ISBN 978-1-4795-6105-6 (paper over board)
  ISBN 978-1-4795-6109-4 (eBook PDF)
1. Crabs—Migration—Christmas Island (Indian Ocean)—Juvenile
literature. 2. Crabs—Behavior—Juvenile literature. 3. Animal
migration—Juvenile literature. I. Wald, Christina, illustrator. II. Title. III.
Title: Christmas Island crab migration.
  QL444.M33K38 2015
  595.3'86—dc23   2014024414

Printed in the United States of America in North Mankato, Minnesota.
102014   008482CGS15

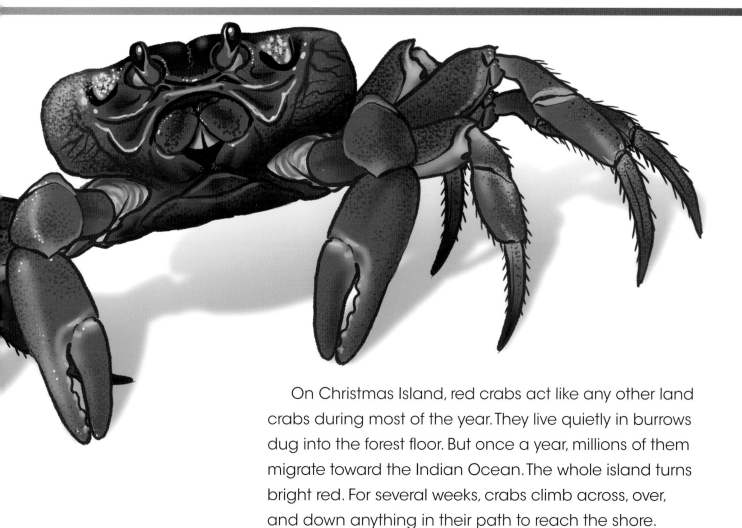

On Christmas Island, red crabs act like any other land crabs during most of the year. They live quietly in burrows dug into the forest floor. But once a year, millions of them migrate toward the Indian Ocean. The whole island turns bright red. For several weeks, crabs climb across, over, and down anything in their path to reach the shore. Why is this journey so important to them?

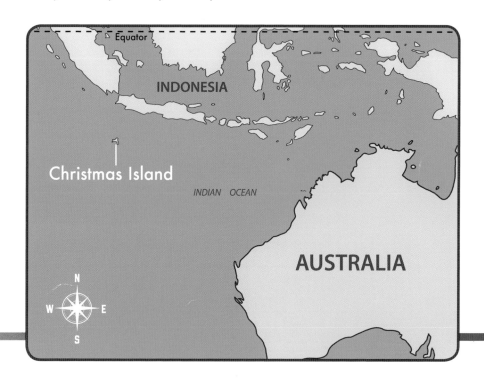

Drip, drop! Drip, drop! The sound of rain wakes up the red crab. She stretches and waves her claws. She hasn't moved for a long time. During the dry winter months, she slept, tucked safe inside her moist burrow.

Now the rainy season begins. The red crab clears the opening to her burrow. *Clomp!* Another red crab almost steps on her. *Clomp! Clomp!* Dozens of red crabs skitter by. They are all walking in the same direction. They are heading toward the beach.

The red crab feels the need to follow them. The beach is far away for an animal her size. The long, dangerous journey will take more than one week.

Along the way she climbs over rocks and fallen trees. She stops to eat leaves and seeds. She crosses roads and barely misses being hit by a car.

The red crab comes to a steep cliff. But it does not stop her. She climbs down quickly. Thousands upon thousands of crabs crawl alongside her.

The crabs have been walking for just over one week. The air outside the forest is drier than inside their burrows. They need to stay wet or they will die. Where is the beach?

There it is! The Indian Ocean! The red crab scurries in.

After a dip in the water, the red crab walks back up the beach. Quick as a blink, two claws grab her. It's a male crab. He arrived first to get his beach burrow ready for her. The two crabs crawl inside the burrow and mate. Once they've mated the male heads back to the forest. The female stays behind. She has important work to do.

The red crab watches the moon. She watches the tide. When the time is right, she leaves the sandy burrow and runs to the water. Raising her claws above her, she does a little dance. She shakes her body up and down to drop thousands of eggs into the ocean. Hundreds of other female red crabs do the same thing.

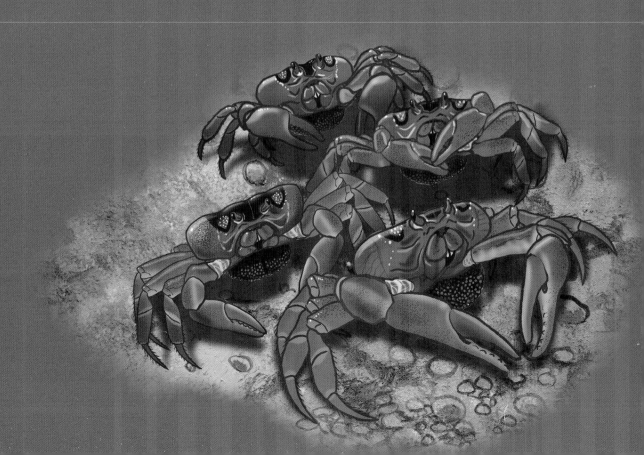

As soon as the red crab's eggs hit the water, two things happen. First, her job is done. The red crab heads back to the forest the way she came. Second, all the eggs hatch! Millions of tiny crab larvae swirl around in the water. Crab babies must hatch in seawater. This fact is why the red crabs made such long journeys.

The larvae grow in the ocean for about one month. Fish gobble up many of them. The lucky larvae change into tiny baby crabs no bigger than pencil erasers. They leave the ocean by the millions and turn the whole water's edge red.

The tiny red crabs head toward the forest.
No one tells them where to go. They just know.
They will spend the next four or five years
hiding between rocks and under leaves.

Then they too will take part in
the amazing red crab migration.

Christmas Island Crab Fast Facts

Scientific name: *Gecarcoidea natalis*

Full-grown size (about 4 to 5 years old): carapace about 4.5 inches (11 centimeters) wide

Home: Christmas Island, a territory of Australia, off the northwestern coast of Australia, near the equator

Eggs: females lay up to 100,000 eggs at a time; egg-laying happens before the morning of the high tide that comes before the December new moon

Diet: fallen leaves, seeds, fruit, snails, dead animals, human trash

Life span: about 20 to 30 years

Natural predators: none on Christmas Island; young are eaten by fish and other animals in the ocean

Main threat: climate change; Christmas Island crabs will not migrate or mate if too little rain falls, putting them in danger of dying out

Migration: around 50 million crabs take part; the only species of land crabs where both males and females migrate

Dig Deeper

1. Why is it important for millions of Christmas Island crabs to go to the beach each year?

2. Describe the dangers Christmas Island crabs face on their migration journey.

3. What does the inset on page 18 show? Why does the illustrator use an inset?

Glossary

burrow—a tunnel or hole in the ground made or used by an animal to live in

carapace—a hard shell that covers the main part of a crab's body

climate—the average weather conditions of a place throughout the year

equator—an imaginary line around the middle of Earth

high tide—the farthest inland that ocean water reaches on the coast

larva—a stage in development between an egg and an adult; the word for more than one larva is "larvae"

mate—to join together to produce young

migrate—to move from one area to another on a regular basis, usually to find food or to produce young

tide—the daily rising and falling of the ocean's water level

Read More

Berkes, Marianne. *Going Home: The Mystery of Animal Migration.* Nevada City, Calif.: Dawn Publications, 2010.

Marsh, Laura. *Amazing Animal Journeys.* Great Migrations. Washington, D.C.: National Geographic, 2010.

Nelson, Robin. *Migration.* Discovering Nature's Cycles. Minneapolis: Lerner, 2011.

Index

About the Author

Sharon Katz Cooper is a science educator and freelance writer who specializes in science and social studies topics. She has written more than 25 books for children, including a series called Horrible Habitats, which was recommended by the National Science Teachers Association (NSTA). She is based in Pittsburgh, Penn., where she lives with her husband and three boys, Reuven, Judah, and Yaron.

About the Illustrator

Christina Wald has done illustration for a wide variety of toys, games, books, and magazines—everything from board books and pop-up books to Star Wars role-playing games and G.I. Joe package art. She studied Industrial Design at the University of Cincinnati. When she is not in the studio, Christina is out urban sketching, biking, and/or traveling. She lives in Cincinnati with her toy engineer husband, Troy, and two cats.

LOOK FOR ALL THE BOOKS IN THE SERIES:

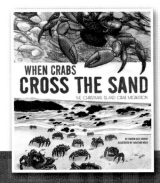

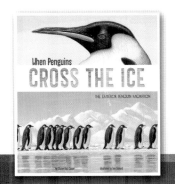

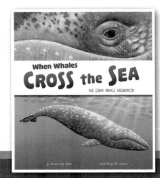